solving conflict nonviolently

Atrium Publications
PO Box 938
Ojai, CA 93023

(alphabetically)

Illustrations:	Rod Cameron
Coordinator:	Kathy DesPrez
Cover Design:	Robert Howard
Design & Production:	Charlene Koonce
Editor:	Adryan Russ
Advisor:	John Shoolery
Word Processing:	I'm Your Type
Creative Consultant:	Jean Webster-Doyle

Special Thanks to Julietta, my thirteen year old stepdaughter,
who felt it was important to write this book for young people.

ISBN: 0-942941-21-7
ISBN: 0-942941-20-9 (Pbk.)

TUG OF WAR

PEACE THROUGH UNDERSTANDING CONFLICT

by Terrence Webster-Doyle

Atrium Publications
Ojai, California

This book is dedicated to you young people who feel the urgency to bring about peace on earth. This book is also dedicated to parents, teachers, counselors and administrators who want to help young people understand what prevents peace — in other words, how to resolve conflict intelligently and nonviolently.

Table of Contents

WHAT DO YOU KNOW ABOUT YOUR BRAIN?

Your Five Senses: Input Center

What's an orange? Have you ever seen one? Have you touched one? Tasted one? If you have one where you are, pick it up and look at it. How is it like a carrot, or different from an apple? Is an orange similar to a grapefruit? How would you describe an orange to someone who had never seen one before?

The best way to answer these questions and understand the meaning of an orange is to see one and hold it in your hand. You know, from direct experience, that an orange is a particular color, shape, size and flavor. If, however, you had never seen an orange, you could create a mental picture of it based on words I use to describe one to you. You would create that mental picture using thought.

Well, that's the way I'm hoping you'll read this book — using (1) direct experience and (2) thought.

Direct experience is what you get by using your five senses — seeing, hearing, touching, tasting and smelling:

The orange is round and orange in color. It's rough to the touch, and has a fruity aroma. The inside is pulpy, with seeds. It's tangy-sweet and juicy.

Thought is how you review the information you've learned from direct experience:

This fruit is a lighter orange color than a carrot. It's smaller than a grapefruit, but has the same kind of rough skin. It's about the same size as an apple, but an apple has smooth skin and is red, green or yellow.

Your five senses give you messages about people, places and things. They allow you to become familiar with your environment. By seeing, touching, smelling, tasting and feeling, you take in all there is to know about the world around you. If you think of your body as a computer, your five senses provide you with all your input.

Your Brain: Command Center

Through your senses you send messages to your brain, the command center of the body. Your brain receives those messages and stores the information in memory. Like a computer, your memory is big enough to store many different kinds of information.

Your brain not only receives and stores information, it sorts it out. That's what *thought* does. It organizes the knowledge your brain accumulates so that you can make use of it. Your brain sorts out your thoughts, enabling you to (1) make certain decisions and (2) take certain actions. These decisions and actions are based on what you need as a human being to survive. You want to survive *physically* (which is why you need rest, healthy food and exercise), and *psychologically* (which is why you need to think healthy thoughts and feel healthy feelings).

Your Thoughts and Actions: Output Center

Everything you think and do in your life is based on your instinct for survival. Your brain works with your body to provide you with what you need to survive and to protect you from harm. That's why, when you believe you are facing danger, whether physical or psychological, you instantly prepare to defend yourself — usually with a reaction known as the "fight or flight response." This means you either (1) fight or (2) run away.

Survival for humans can include a third response: responding intelligently, without fighting or running away. This response is what this book is about.

Your brain is like a giant corporation with many offices; each office has a different, yet related, function to help you survive and live a healthy, happy life. However, your computer-like brain is also capable of turning into a machine that creates tremendous conflict and produces devastating war. It can create small conflicts (say, for example, between you and your parents), or international conflicts (between nations, producing great suffering).

This book was written to show you how your brain can cause war. It is my hope that by reading it you will understand how we create conflict in our daily lives, and how certain thoughts and actions can create conflict in the world. I believe that this kind of understanding is what will lead us to peace.

As you read this book, exploring the boundaries of your inner space, searching for truth:

1. Stay with it — follow all your leads, like a detective solving a mystery;
2. Be cool and calm, like a Karate Master using his mind to end a battle before it begins; and
3. Ask questions until your curiosity is satisfied. Asking questions turns on a light in an otherwise dark corner of your mind.

The Saber-Toothed Tiger's Revenge
A Story

The roar of the saber-toothed tiger rang ferociously in the dead black night. Human-like creatures huddled nervously in the small cave, their eyes alert. They grunted fearful sounds, in voices not loud enough for their predator to hear. The moon shone brightly on the thick undergrowth. The beast was coming closer, its scent in the air.

One of the human creatures started to move in panic. The others tried to stop this one from revealing their hiding place. Suddenly, the frightened one ran out of the shallow cave into the night, shrieking in terror. As this human creature tried to gain higher ground and reach the tall trees to climb for safety, out of the dense blackness, a sudden leaping, fanged beast grabbed the human creature by the neck. The scream sent terror into the rest of the human creatures huddled in their temporary hiding place. Again, another of their group had been taken to its brutal and violent death.

Dawn came and there was no beast in sight. The air was damp with primeval mist. Large birds flew overhead, screeching primitive calls, causing smaller prey on the ground to scurry into hiding for fear of attack.

The human creatures moved slowly and carefully out of hiding, sniffing the air for danger. These dark, stooped, hairy creatures half-walked, half-crawled out into the new day.

Grunting noises of anticipation and alarm, the creatures cautiously crept toward the large water hole beyond the dense forest. Coming upon the water, the creatures suddenly charged down the small hill, shrieking as they descended. Smaller animals looked up quickly from their drinking and ran for the cover of the trees and the safety of their shelters.

The human creatures stood almost totally erect and made threats with their arms, waving them at the retreating animals. After some cautious scouting, the small group sat down on their haunches to drink the cool water, all the time carefully watching the edge of the forest for any intruders.

For a long while, these human creatures dominated this survival area, keeping on guard against any surprises. Sitting by the bank of the watering hole, they picked up small bits of grass and leaves, smelling and tasting each sample of wild growing plant.

Later in the morning, the group moved slowly off into the thick underbrush in search of more edibles. Coming upon a clearing, they found huge buzzards eating the flesh of a great elephant-like creature recently killed by an even larger animal. This half-eaten beast had attracted hungry scavengers who were fighting over the remains. The human creatures ran toward the scavenging animals, screaming and driving them away from the food. They waved their arms, threw rocks, and challenged the others with sticks.

A saber-toothed cat and her two cubs were temporarily driven off. Meanwhile, a small pack of hyenas tried to close in to regain their prey. Even though the human creatures were smaller and no match for the saber-toothed cat and hyenas, they managed, by working together as a tribe, to keep the larger and fiercer animals from their dinner. Perhaps this would be the last full meal eaten by the human creatures for a long time.

They ate greedily, while anxiously watching the other hungry animals — all of whom, given the chance, would kill them to get at the food. While they ate, they hunched down in a protective circle, cautiously remaining alert to any movement on all sides around them. They ate as fast as they could because the sun was falling, and at night there was always the chance that a powerful beast of prey — like the saber-toothed tiger — would make dinner out of *them*.

Chapter 1

EARTHLINGS:
CREATURES WHO FIGHT TO SURVIVE

It's hard to believe that modern man was once the ape-like creature in the story you just read. It has taken about 10 million years for this evolution. We are not the creatures we were then, but in many ways we are still the same:

1. **We protect our families**. ("Be careful crossing the street!")
2. **We are territorial**. ("Tell Ted not to play with *my* toys!")
3. **We compete with other members of our own species**. ("You're *wrong*, and I'm *right*!")

Today, many of the things we say and do every day are based on that same instinct: Survival.

The Past: Survival Meant Fighting

Throughout history, when supplies (such as food, water and shelter) have been limited, we humans have fought each other over them. Thousands of years ago, when man lived in isolated tribes, these tribes had to hunt and kill animals for food in order to survive. Sometimes lack of rain caused drought and intense heat caused fire, killing the plants that animals needed to eat. All living creatures would then have to move on to find water and food. Sometimes one tribe would wander into the hunting grounds of another tribe, and this would cause *war* between them. They fought wars then for *biological* reasons: they were hungry, thirsty and cold, and they needed food and shelter to survive.

The Present: Man is Still Fighting

Man has created a highly organized system of survival, and we have invented extraordinary machines to do much of our work. Today, we produce huge quantities of food, and house millions of people. But we are still fighting. Do you think that we are fighting today because of biological reasons?

We still have tribes: the American tribe, the Russian tribe, the African tribe, the Japanese tribe, the Catholic, Jewish, Buddhist and Communist tribes. Each tribe takes care of, and is mainly concerned about, its own people. When one tribe wanders into the territory of another without permission, sometimes they go to war. Do you think that we still war for biological reasons?

I think that our present-day "tribes" fight because they want to survive, but today they fight for *psychological* reasons rather than biological ones. Instead of fighting over food and shelter, we fight over who can buy the *most* food, or own the *best* house. Rather than share land, we fight over who is *entitled* to it. Rather than learn about what beliefs are, we insist that our beliefs are "right" and those of others are "wrong." Because of these battles, we continue to kill millions of our own kind. Modern man, with all his technology, is still very primitive.

The Future:
Survival Means Not Fighting

Isn't it amazing that we still belong to tribes that fight — my school against your school, my town against your town, my country against your country? We all want to survive, and if we plan to survive in centuries to come, we're going to have to make some changes in how we live with one another. In the past, man had to fight in order to survive. Today, our survival depends on *not* fighting.

Technology is advancing so quickly that communication between today's tribes is immediate. With telephones, fax machines and video capabilities, one part of the world can be in contact with any other part of the world — instantly. This creates the feeling of little or no distance between us.

When astronauts first travelled to the moon in 1969 and took photographs of earth, we saw the world — many of us for the first time — as a whole. All of our streams, lakes and oceans swirled into and out of one another, and there was no indication in those photos of where one country ended and another began. Those pictures showed us what we truly are: a single planet of people whirling around in space — together.

We are really one global tribe, and yet we continue to be divided through tribal associations and, therefore, we're still at war. Because we have tribes (nations), we have war.

Chapter 2

CONFLICT IS WAR

If you want to watch television, but your parents want you to do homework, there is conflict between you. When your friend wants to go bicycle riding, but you want to see a movie, there is conflict between you.

Conflict is what happens when there is disagreement. It's a war that happens in our minds. It can start out small and disappear, or it can start out small and grow into a major war. How we handle conflict determines how things will turn out.

The Structure of Conflict

Every conflict has a basic structure, like a house. You know that a house has an inner structure — a foundation, a frame and a roof — which determines how the outer structure is going to look. The inner structure of our conflict, composed of the causes, determines how the conflict will be expressed. If, for example, someone hurts your feelings and you get angry, your hurt feelings are the cause of your anger.

Just as the outer structure of a house is the result of the inner structure, the outer structures of conflict — called *symptoms* — are the result of the causes. Using the above example, your anger is the *symptom* of your hurt feelings. In any conflict situation, most of us see the symptom but don't always see the cause. Looking at the cause helps us understand the conflict.

When was the last time you were in conflict with someone? Do you recall what the disagreement was about?

1. What did you want? What did the other person want?
2. What did the other person say that may have caused the disagreement?
3. What did you say that may have *caused* it?
4. Did you *think* about what you were saying?
5. Did you *listen* to the other person's point of view? What was it? (Was she/he disappointed? Sad? Angry?)
6. Do you think this feeling was a *symptom* of what he/she wanted?
7. What do you think was the *cause* of this feeling?
8. If the conflict was starting now, would you say anything different? Why? Why not?

These questions can be helpful to you in any disagreement you have with a friend, a family member, even yourself. Paying attention to what you want, what the other person wants, what you said, what the other person said — these are all important in understanding conflict.

Conflict is No Holiday

One night I was walking around my neighborhood after midnight. I live in a small town where it's safe to walk at night. The streets were quiet and the air sweet with the scents of spring. The moon shone brightly and there was a deep silence. I enjoy walking when everyone is asleep. There is more opportunity for understanding when the brain is quiet.

14

While walking, I was aware of how peaceful it was. There was no conflict, no violence. It was as if everyone had gone on holiday. It suddenly dawned on me that war ends when people go to sleep! I was awakened early the next morning by the violent sound of cars — metal boxes driven by people fighting each other in traffic lanes on their way to spending eight or ten or more hours fighting each other in competitive lives. The holiday was over.

That's when I realized that conflict is an everyday event. Sometimes schools are a battlefield: students fight amongst themselves or with school authorities. Sometimes the workplace is a battlefield: employees fight with employers or each other. We fight to be first in line or to get a parking place. Sometimes we fight to get compensated or recognized for our work. Life sometimes seems like one big fight.

Conflict Causes Separation

The main problem with fighting is that it causes separation. It tears people apart instead of bringing them together. If we're ever going to get people to come together, we're going to have to cease fighting. And the only way we can do this is to learn to understand why we fight in the first place.

A conflict between you and a friend, and a conflict between Russia and the United States are not much different. If you can understand what has caused conflict between you and your friend, then you can *understand* why the U.S. and Russia might disagree. To help us reach that understanding, the section that follows begins with a story, "Through the Eyes of Peace," in which a young girl sees peace where none seems to exist. This story shows that what you see is what you get.

Through the Eyes of Peace
A Story

Representatives of two countries were standing in a large hall in a major city in the United States. They had come from far away, from lands that were at war. Their countries had been battling for centuries — the same war over and over, family after family dying for the same cause: Freedom. As far back as recorded history goes, they had been at war with each other.

Now they were face-to-face in the same space. They began walking nervously around the room. They were meeting without their usual weapons and uniforms, and it was hard to recognize who was who without their military regalia. No one had rank. No one wore medals. They were dressed in similar clothing — shirts, pants, jackets in the style of the United States or Europe.

But neither side saw their similarities. They only saw their differences. And they argued in the great hall.

"*You* are the terrorists! *We* are the freedom fighters!" one side would say.

"No, no! *We* are the freedom fighters! *You* are the terrorists!" the other side would retort.

They were rattling off rapid, anxious words — like machine gun bullets.

"It is *our* claimed Holy Land. Our Holy Scriptures tell us that this land is *ours.*"

"*We* are the Chosen Ones!" the other side would reply.

"No! Our forefathers were here before yours. See, it says so in our Holy Book. God is on *our* side!"

"Your God is false. Our God is the only true God!" the other side shouted back in anger. "Anyone not believing that the land belongs to us is the enemy and must die!"

"No, no. Our law says that *you* are the enemy!"

And on and on they went for weeks in these "negotiations," discussions designed to generate an agreement. But there was no agreement.

There was world news coverage of the goings on. "Experts" interviewed both sides, then wrote news reports and best selling books on the subject. These experts spoke on television, radio, at colleges and universities, discussing complicated reasons why the negotiations were not working. They were rewarded with money and honors around the world for their analysis. In the meantime, however, the arguing continued and the war went on.

One day a young girl visited the negotiations with her father, who was in military service. This was her first time, and she was surprised by all the arguing.

"Daddy, why are they so afraid of each other?" she asked.

"They're not afraid," her father said, embarrassed by her comment.

"What are they shouting about?" she inquired.

"Each one believes in their God and their country, and they are trying to solve the problems of war," the father replied.

"Oh," said the girl. "I thought they hated each other."

"Oh, no, they are trying not to be enemies."

"How could they be enemies," asked the girl, "when they look and sound exactly alike?"

Chapter 3

OUR CONDITIONING
CAN CAUSE WAR

The young girl in the previous story could see that the representatives of the two countries were the same in many ways. In her eyes, they had every reason to be friends. The representatives, however, saw only their differences and believed they were enemies. How could two perceptions of the same situation be so different? The answer is: Conditioning.

What is Conditioning?

In daily life, we are influenced by our surroundings. This influencing is "conditioning." We are conditioned to brush our teeth every day; we are conditioned to cross the street on a green light, to stop for a red light; we are conditioned to applaud "heroes" or "heroines" and to boo "villains."

Conditioning means we've been *taught to think* in certain ways. At home, for example, you are conditioned to think and act the way your family does. At school, your teachers and friends have an influence on your thoughts and actions. If you are taking a Karate class, you are conditioned by the principles taught there and by the people in your class. Each group offers ways to think and act that each considers "right" or "good." We are taught these ways because our friends and family believe they are appropriate and will help us survive; we act in those ways because we want to please the people around us.

When people have different ideas about what is "right" or "good," there is division. Conditioning creates beliefs and beliefs separate people, causing conflict individually and globally. In the story, "Through the Eyes of Peace," two nations had different beliefs which put them in opposition to each other. However, there is another type of division which happens inside one person when that person belongs to two different groups that disagree. That division is called internal conflict.

Individual Example:

You and your friends want to learn Karate. However, your family doesn't want you to take lessons because they are afraid you'll get hurt. This difference between you and your parents can cause you great conflict. You want to join your friends and learn Karate, but you don't want to disobey your parents. Your parents have been conditioned by the media to think that all Karate is violent, but you and your friends see that the type of Karate you want to learn is not violent and is helpful.

Global Example:

One "group" (tribe, nation) of people identifies with a particular way of life through certain forms of ritual handed down over centuries. They come into contact with other "groups" who identify with different, and perhaps opposed, ways of living. Each group has been conditioned to think of themselves as special. Yet *all* the people are human beings. But because they have separated themselves by having different beliefs, they are in conflict. One group (tribe, nation, sect) says that, "*Mine* is the right way! *We* are the selected ones!" And the other groups say the same thing. So who is right and who is wrong? Can every group be "right"? Can every group be the "selected one"?

Where does conditioning start? When we are small children, our parents may insist that we go to bed at a certain time. Perhaps they need the evening to themselves, or they know we must get up early in the morning and we need the sleep. Parents don't always reveal their reasons, but they "condition" us to conform to certain habits.

As we grow up, we are conditioned to do many things — some which protect us from harm ("Look both ways before crossing the street!"), and some which are supposed to be for our own good ("Finish all the food on your plate!").

We are asked to clean our rooms, be kind to other people, and do what we're told. Some adults feel that these actions make us "good" children. So, through the years, we are conditioned to be "good" — and we continue trying to be "good."

Doing what we are told may start out as "positive" conditioning, but it may not end up that way. For instance, finishing our food is something parents want us to do, but doing it all the time could cause obesity or illness. You know, better than anyone, how much food your body can take in.

Being friendly towards people is "positive" behavior — something most of us are taught to do — but there is such a thing as being friendly to the wrong people. If we are conditioned to *always* be friendly to people, that could cause great conflict should we run into someone who intends to harm us. Or, if we feel we should be friendly even when we don't feel like it, we experience conflict.

Conditioning starts when we are very young — when we are first rewarded or punished for our behavior. Our parents, teachers, religious and political leaders all want us to act in certain ways. Being "good" can mean being a good American or a good Russian, a good Christian, Catholic, Buddhist, or Jew. So being "good" means acting according to the particular thinking (beliefs) of the particular society we live in. If you are raised a Jew in Russia and I am raised a Christian in America, then we are divided by our different beliefs.

Being "good" is acting the way we think we *should*, and the way we should behave is formed by our beliefs; our beliefs form our attitudes and our attitudes create our actions. If we have the attitude that "our way" is better or superior to others, then we are essentially creating war.

The Only Behavior We Know

For many of us, conflict/war is the only behavior we know. The reason? It's everywhere we look. Living in today's complex world means living in constant conflict. We are surrounded by conflict and have been conditioned to accept war as the honorable solution to conflict.

1. Every day on news broadcasts, there are depictions of war somewhere in the world, or family conflicts in which parents and children hurt one another.
2. Movie theaters and television feature war movies.
3. War comics on newsstands are filled with violence.
4. Crime and drugs seem to be everywhere.
5. Toy stores carry what they call "action toys" consisting of

every kind of weapon you can imagine: pistols, rifles, machine guns, cannons, tanks, fighter planes, knives, and other tools of destruction.
6. Video arcades feature games that are like miniature wars. (Did you know that real wars are run by computers very much like the ones in arcades?)

Remember when we discussed how what you see is what you get? Well, do you think that it's possible that watching war movies conditions some people to want to go to war? If kids see toy weapons for sale, and read comic books that show people killing each other, do you think that they begin to believe that violence is acceptable?

Until now, you might not have thought very much about your conditioning. You act in a certain way because that's the only behavior you know. In the pages that follow, you will have the opportunity to examine your behavior to find out if it's causing you conflict — and to change it, if you want to.

How Are We Conditioned?

You now know that we believe in certain things because we've been "conditioned" to believe in them. People condition us, and we condition others. But do you know how we do this?

If you have a dog, you probably know you can "condition" the dog to roll over by offering a biscuit. The dog rolls over because it wants the treat; this treat is the dog's *reward*. A dog can also be conditioned by *punishment*. If you take the dog's treat away, you can also condition it to do what you want; in order to get the treat back, the dog will obey.

24

When we want *people* to act in a certain way, we do the same thing. We either reward or punish them. We offer them love, or we take our love away. We offer them gifts, or we threaten them. We are kind to them, or we show our anger.

When you were very small, your parents rewarded you for the simplest things. For example, they gave you love and attention when you smiled. When they didn't want you to touch something, they may have frowned at you and said, "No!" in a loud, angry voice. That was "punishment" for doing something they didn't want you to do.

The Pleasure of Rewards

When I think of rewards, I think of chocolate ice cream, a trip to a favorite place, a special gift, or a special friendship. Have you ever offered anyone a reward for doing something for you? Has anyone offered you a reward for something you've done? What was it? Think a moment about the reward and how you felt when you got it. Did it condition you to do the same thing again in order to get the reward?

The Pain of Punishment

When I think of punishment, I think of physical attack, threats, name calling, or words that are hurtful. Have you ever used punishment to get something? Has anyone ever used punishment to get you to do something for them? What kind? Punishment can also be a lack of behavior — such as *not* talking to you, *not* taking you to the movies, or *not* letting you go to a party. Did the punishment you received condition you to do or *not* do something again?

Questions:

1. Have you been conditioned to do certain things?
2. What things have you been conditioned to do?
3. Why do you think you've been conditioned to do them?
4. Would you reward a friend for doing you a favor? How would you do it?
5. Would you punish someone for hurting your feelings? How would you do it?
6. Name one activity you have been conditioned to do that makes you feel good.
7. Name one activity you have been conditioned to do that does not make you feel good.
8. In what ways does conditioning create global conflict?
9. In what ways have you been conditioned to separate yourself from other human beings?
10. What beliefs do you have?
    A. Religious? B. National?
11. Do these beliefs bring you together with people?
12. Can beliefs create a whole, undivided world?

Remember — not all conditioning creates conflict. Some conditioning is necessary to help us survive — like crossing the street in a marked area. However, another type of conditioning, that we are not always aware of, divides and separates people into opposing groups and creates conflict. This book will help you see the difference between constructive (or healthy) conditioning and destructive (or unhealthy) conditioning, conditioning that can create war.

Chapter 4

THE ROOTS OF WAR

Because of our conditioning, we've all been *hurt*, both physically and emotionally, and that hurt causes us to feel conflict. Because we don't like the way it feels to be in conflict, we condition our brains to protect us. Being in conflict is a threat to our survival. No matter where we go or what we do, that ever present instinct to survive stays with us.

Sometimes a single thought can cause us conflict, because the thought reminds us of another time when we were hurt or scared. There are times when even a single word will cause conflict in us. It hurts our feelings, frightens us, makes us feel "bad" or "wrong."

War Begins With One, But It Takes Two

As small and minor as this kind of conflict seems, it can easily blow up into a full-fledged war. War begins with one human being. A person may not be aware that he or she is starting it, but that's how it begins. You know that in any disagreement you've had with family or friends, the pattern goes something like this:

1. Someone says or does something that sparks negative (hurtful) feelings inside you. For example, they might say: **"How could you do a stupid thing like that?"**

2. The word "stupid" creates conflict inside you. You feel "wrong," "bad" or dumb. You're hurt, perhaps angry. These feelings make you want to "get back" at the person. These "get back at" thoughts are violent, and violent thoughts can lead to violent actions. When they do, your violent feelings can come out as violent words. You respond: **"Not as stupid as you! What are *you* using for a brain?"**

3. The other person, not realizing he has hurt your feelings, suddenly feels "attacked." He thinks, "What does that mean, 'What am I using for a brain?' What's the matter with that idiot? I hate smart mouths." These are also violent thoughts. His violent thoughts lead *him* to violent words: **"At least I *have* a brain, moron. What's *your* excuse?"**

4. The war is on.

A war is always started by a point of view, but it takes more than one to make a war.

The same goes for internal wars. It takes two opposing thoughts to create a war in your brain. If you have a single thought ("I want to work after school to earn money"), there is no conflict. But if you have two conflicting thoughts ("I want to work after school to earn money, but if I do, my grades might suffer"), the mental tug of war is on.

How Important is Winning?

Once involved in a war, whether physical or mental, each side is geared to "win." It's that old survival instinct again. And if one side wins, it follows that the other has to lose. That is the nature of war — there is a winner and a loser.

We human beings think that in order to achieve success, we must fight to win. We turn our lives into a 24-hour a day sporting event. Schools set up contests to get students to *compete* with one another for the best grades or the most recognition. They say this type of competition is healthy and encourages students to work harder.

Business offices encourage competition among co-workers. They offer salary increases, bonuses and vacations as prizes for getting *prime* customers, selling the *most* products, creating the *best* advertising campaign. Employees are encouraged to take business away from others, or get someone else's job. (People who find executive jobs for other people are called "Head Hunters" — even sounds primitive!)

Think for a moment about a time when *you* witnessed competition.

1. Do you see competition at school or at home?
2. What kind of competition have you seen at school?
3. What kind of competition happens between you and someone at home?
4. Are there healthy kinds of competition that can help you grow stronger?
5. Are there unhealthy kinds of competition that cause conflict between people?

6. Remember how human creatures fought in primeval times? What were they competing for?
7. Do you see similarities between fights you have with your family and fights that went on between primitive creatures?

What Can We Learn from Losing?

We love to win and we hate to lose. Most of us are taught to be "good," to be "the best," to do well, and to work hard to succeed. Sometimes we are afraid that if we don't do well, if we don't "succeed," someone may not like us, or someone may deprive us of certain privileges. Adults are sometimes scared that someone will take away their business, their job, their future. If they lose their job, how will they pay their bills, keep the house, take care of you?

Have you ever thought about why *you* don't like to lose? I know I don't like the feeling of losing because it makes me feel I have done something "wrong," that I've failed, or that I'm not as good as I could be. When I "lose," I'm sometimes afraid that someone will think I'm "bad" or "incompetent." It's like being called "stupid."

How about you? When you are competing — in sports or on a spelling test — are you afraid of losing?

1. What would happen if you played an important game and you lost?
2. How would you feel?
3. Would you be afraid? If so, of what?

There is a lot to be learned from losing. When you lose, you learn what you *didn't* do. The experience of losing teaches you to start over and approach your goal from a different point of view. New points of view often help you reach an understanding of what you can do next time that will be better. If you are conditioned to play a game a certain way and you lose, you may discover a new way to play that will improve your game.

Have you ever listened to professional athletes after they've lost a game? They become analytical and philosophical. They look at how they played, they *analyze* what they did that might have influenced the loss, they *think about* how their opponents played, and they work on making their game stronger next time. Winning feels great, but you don't learn half as much.

Questions:

1. What memories do you have of winning in your life? How did you feel when you won? What did you learn?
2. What memories do you have of losing? How did you feel when you lost? What did you learn?

Activity:

Talk to people about winning and losing. Ask them how they felt when they lost a game or an argument. Make two lists: (1) Things People Learned From Winning, and (2) Things People Learned From Losing. See how they compare.

Remember:

Look and see if you can discover the root of war within you. Are you different from other people? Don't all human beings basically react the same way? Don't we all suffer, feel hurt, and protect ourselves from being hurt?

So, when we look at ourselves, we are looking at the whole human race. If I am hurt and defend myself out of that hurt, isn't it probable that all humans do the same? So "my" hurt is your hurt; the individual hurt is the whole human race's hurt. Also, if I react with anger and self-protectiveness from "my hurt," do you think that nations (large groups of people) react in the same way? If I strike out from that anger and punch you because you have hurt me, do you think that countries — with human leaders — do the same? Isn't the root of war in us all? Knowing this, we can approach the issue of war and peace in a very different and more creative way.

If we understand why we get hurt and what causes us to defend against it, we will see the roots of conflict within each of us and how these internal roots create disorder and violence in the world.

Chapter 5

OUR THOUGHTS AND ACTIONS CAN CAUSE WAR

How you think about me (or others) is going to determine how you act toward me (or others). If we meet on the street and you think I have done you harm, there are three basic ways you can respond:

1. If you are angry and *believe* you should fight me, then you may try to do so.
2. If you are angry but *believe* you should not fight, then you may walk the other way.
3. If I *see* your anger and understand that it's a symptom of conflict going on inside you, I may ask, "Why are you angry?" If we wind up talking about why you are angry, I may find out that I accidentally hurt your feelings, and I may apologize; then you may apologize for flying off the handle. (We may even discuss why people get hurt because we want to get to the cause of the problem.)

The solution to conflict depends on what we think, how we act, and what we say to each other.

Many human beings believe that the only way to resolve conflict is to fight. They have been conditioned to believe this by their families and friends, or by so-called "experts" who insist that we *need* to fight wars and spend billions of dollars on war machinery and military weapons in order to keep the peace.

I believe that what we need more than anything is to develop an *understanding* of why human beings feel the need to fight. That need begins with our thinking.

Conflicts begin because of the way we think.
The way we think determines the way we act.

The "Fight or Flight" Response

Can you remember the last time you were frightened of someone or something? Maybe it was a scary movie, or creaking noises late at night. Perhaps a bully cornered you in the schoolyard. Take a moment to think about the last time you felt scared of someone or something.

1. When was it?
2. What were you afraid of?

Your thinking at the time caused you to take some action. More than likely, you either decided to (1) fight, or (2) run away. All beings have this built-in instinct whenever they are faced with conflict.

In the story of "The Saber-Toothed Tiger's Revenge" at the beginning of this book, the primitive creatures either *fought* for food and shelter, or they *ran away*. Today, this fight or flight mechanism is still inside us: Do we fight the bully in the schoolyard, or do we run away? Do we fight for what we believe, or give up? Do we "fight it out" in our job, or quit and go to another one? Do we fight another country over who gets a certain piece of land, or do we go away and let them have it?

How Our Survival is Threatened

We make the decision to fight or run away based on our instinct to survive. When we get involved in an argument or a physical fight, our survival is threatened. We decide, on the spot, if we're going to stay and fight, or if we're going to run. There is no "good" or "bad" decision: it's a matter of survival.

There are other ways our survival can be threatened. If we don't get enough rest, eat healthy food, or exercise, our health may weaken and our physical body may get sick. Most of us have a basic idea of what we need to do to keep our physical selves healthy.

Our emotional and mental selves are important too. The way we maintain our psychological self is to think healthy thoughts and feel healthy feelings. Since our brains are not visible like our bodies, we aren't always aware when our mental self is unhealthy. One way to tell is by feeling inner conflict, because unhealthy thoughts and feelings are the ones that produce conflict.

In our desire to survive, we sometimes avoid conflict producing thoughts and feelings because we feel threatened by them. Our brain "runs away" by creating "escapes" — ways to avoid the conflict. The problem is that these escapes often take us away from the conflict for just a short period of time; if a conflict isn't resolved, it keeps coming back. In addition, when we attempt to hide conflicting feelings, we often wind up creating more. Here are some examples of how this works.

The following are four causes of conflict. They are forms of thought that we use to "escape."

A. Scapegoating.
When our brain scapegoats, it thinks that something outside itself is the cause of its problems. It blames others for its own suffering. "You (person, country, religion, group) are the reason I feel this way." We use that person or thing as a "scapegoat."

B. Prejudice.
Many of us are conditioned to believe that some people are better than others and some people are worse. We pre-judge people because we have an image "stuck" in our brain, and through that prejudiced image, we look at the world. "You (color of skin) people are bad."

C. Stereotyping.
Stereotyping is conditioned thinking that labels and categorizes people. The brain gathers information about one person, then bases its judgment of others in the same group by this one. "You (group of people) are all stupid."

D. Projecting.
Just as a movie is *projected* onto a movie screen, this form of thinking *projects* what we ourselves have said or done onto someone else. Often it's something we don't like in ourselves that we want to get rid of. Our brain accuses others to hide our own feelings of guilt. "You (person, country, religion, group) are the enemy!"

Scapegoating, prejudice, stereotyping and projection are all forms of thinking that *blame* others for thoughts and actions we do not want to accept in ourselves. These thought patterns have gotten lodged in our brains by years of conditioning. Our brains have stored "knowledge" we've gathered — from parents, teachers, radio, television, movies, books and magazines — in our computer-like memories; this knowledge has become so much a part of us that we often can't separate ourselves from it. These thought patterns become our conditioning, our habits, our predictable robot-like ways of acting.

The way to look for this type of thinking in your own brain is to ask yourself if you have ever had thoughts such as:

1. "I've met his type before; you can't trust them."
2. "If *she* had just done her job, we would have won."
3. "People who come from that country don't know anything."

Anytime you put the blame on "him," "her" or "they," instead of looking at what part you played in the situation, you are adding to the conflict. We forget that there are two sides to any conflict and that "I" or "we" are one half of it.

Activity:

You may already know how it feels when someone blames you for something you didn't do. You may also know how it feels to blame someone else for something you did. Sometimes this happens between brothers and sisters, between classmates,

within families, or between "groups." We usually don't mean to hurt anyone when we do it, but sometimes people do get hurt. And as soon as someone is hurt, there's always the potential for war.

Take a moment to think of a time when something you said or did was too painful to admit, so you blamed or *projected* it onto someone else.

1. What was the situation? What did you say?
2. What thoughts were in your mind before you spoke?
3. How did you feel after you had done it? Why?
3. Why do you think people project their feelings onto others?
4. Do you think they are afraid? Of what?
5. How can we help one another when we do this?

Remember earlier when we were discussing how most of us react to conflict by either (1) fighting or (2) running away? "Escape" thinking does both. When we blame someone, it is like starting a fight — in our minds, as well as between that person and ourselves. "Escape" thinking is also running away. When we run away from a problem, we do nothing to resolve the conflict; our chances for reaching an understanding become nonexistent.

Conflict today can be serious. War between countries can involve atom bombs, and when one of those drops, there is no time to fight or run; neither alternative is available. In today's world, we need to resolve conflict before anyone even thinks of using a bomb. If we're going to continue to survive, we're going to have to find a better way to handle our conflicts.

42

I know there is a better way. Actually, you and I have already been exploring this way, little by little — talking about how we think and how we act, looking at our thoughts and actions and sharing them. Can you see how looking at thoughts before we act has the potential to reduce conflict?

Where Peaceful Behavior Begins

I'll bet you know at least one person you would like to see become more peaceful, friendlier, more polite, stronger, more outgoing, quieter, or more something! But the thing is, the only person you can change for sure is YOU. You can tell your friends that you are learning to be a more peaceful person, but you cannot command your friends to do this too, because that would be telling them what to do and how to be, creating rules for them to follow, giving them orders. It is essential for you to remind yourself, from time to time:

All peaceful behavior begins with me.
The first step is to *understand* any conflict
that enters my life.

If I can understand conflict in my life, I can understand conflict in other people's lives. Conflict is conflict! People are people! It's the same for you and me. Understanding the conflict within myself can have an effect on others; therefore others can change if *I* do.

Chapter 6

THE WAY WE USE WORDS
CAN CAUSE WAR

It's difficult to understand conflict if we can't understand what people say. Words describe persons, places and things, and we use them to communicate — to inform and understand one another. If I say a word like "car," and you hear "car," you connect the word with the object in your driveway. Words help us give directions, teach new ideas, explain our thinking and get things done.

Is It a Fact or Is It a Belief?

There are two categories of words that are important for you to be able to tell apart: (1) **facts** and (2) **beliefs**.

Example: The world is round.

At one time people *believed* the world was flat, but since we've explored outer space and seen photographs of the earth, we *know* the world is round. This is a fact.

Example: There is extraterrestrial life.

A belief is something some people mentally accept to be true, even though there may not be absolute certainty. At this time, while many people *believe* extraterrestrial beings exist, many people do not believe that they exist. We cannot call the statement that "extraterrestrial beings exist" a fact. (Although one day maybe we will.)

In order to prevent conflict, it's important to be able to distinguish between a fact and a belief. This is not, however, always easy to do, because we often confuse beliefs with facts.

Example:

Your parents might say to you:

**"If you go to college, you can earn a degree.
Then you'll be able to find a good job."**

The first sentence is a fact: If you go to college, it is certainly possible for you to get a degree. The second sentence is a belief: There is no way to know for certain that you will find a good job.

Your parents may, however, *believe* you will. Perhaps this belief is based on people they know who have graduated from universities and then landed good jobs. The other side of the coin, however, is that there are also people who have gone the college/university route who have not found "good jobs."

When parents and teachers pass their *beliefs* on to us, they don't usually say, "This is not a fact; it's just what I believe." They often express their beliefs as if they are facts. Obviously, such conditioning is misleading. I think that the purpose of going to college is to learn all you can, so as to be better able to understand yourself, other people, and the world around you. Do you think that's a fact or a belief?

"Double-talk/Doublespeak?"

There are times when people intentionally try to confuse us, because: (1) they are doing something they don't want us to know about; (2) they want us to buy what they are selling; or (3) they want to control us. As a result, they use **"double-talk"** or **"doublespeak."**

Double-talk usually makes use of familiar words, but put together in such a way that they are difficult to understand. People using double-talk often use twice as many words as they need to say something to cover up the fact that they are not telling the truth. Real words become unintelligible, meaningless gobbledegook. As a result, we have even more difficulty distinguishing between facts and beliefs.

Have a look at some examples:

1. **"The victim passed away in uncontrolled contact with the ground."** This, believe it or not, means: Someone died in an airplane crash.

2. **"Elizabeth was discovered in a strategic misrepresentation."** This means that Elizabeth was caught in a lie.

Can you see why this kind of language is called "double-talk"? It does the exact opposite of what language is supposed to do. Instead of helping us communicate, it makes it difficult for us to understand what is being said.

Here are are some other examples of "double-talk," along with their meanings.

1. A portable, hand-held communications inscriber (A pencil)
2. A previously distinguished car (A used car)
3. A grief therapist (An undertaker)
4. An attitude adjustment center (A bar)
5. A grain-consuming animal unit (A pig, cow or chicken)
6. A memorial park (A cemetery)
7. Nervous wetness (Sweat)
8. An environmental technician (A janitor)
9. A mobile estate (A house trailer)
10. A plaque removal instrument (A toothbrush)
11. An automotive internist (A car mechanic)
12. Rapid oxidation (Fire)
13. A pupil station (A school desk)
14. The disadvantaged (Poor people)
15. Sub-standard housing (A slum or ghetto)
16. An unlawful deprivation of life (Killing)

Some of these examples are funny, and some are not necessarily "bad." What's important is that you be able to recognize them.

Propaganda

You've seen lots of TV and magazine ads. You know that the purpose of an ad is to get you to buy the product being advertised. Many advertisers say their product is "the best" or that it gives you "more" of something. You have to ask yourself, "More what?" And, "Do I need more of that?" You have to ask yourself if the product is truly "the best." The best for what? And for whom? Some advertisers offer you a "free gift" if you buy their product. The truth is, of course, that if you buy their product, their gift is not free. It's important to be able to *see through* these ads.

This kind of advertising is called **propaganda**. It uses double-talk to get you to believe and act in ways you would not believe or act if you thought the situation out for yourself. When we understand the difference between a fact and a belief, we are not so easily influenced by propaganda.

Double-talk and Propaganda
Block Our Understanding

The clearest understanding of life comes from **direct observation** and from **thinking**. Remember that in the opening of this book, we talked about how our five senses provide us with input about the world around us. Double-talk and propaganda dull our senses; they take away the reality or feeling of a situation. An "uncontrolled contact with the ground" makes an airplane crash seem unreal and emotionless. The result is that we do not register what has really happened.

"Double-talk/doublespeak" puts us to sleep, because we don't understand it. The danger is that the people who use this misleading language do it with such authority that we don't question it. We think, "They are *specialists* — they must know

48

best." We are confused and blinded, and we begin to doubt our own common sense and ability to understand. Be aware of the groups that use this non-language. The media (television, radio, newspapers, books and magazines) are often users. Sometimes so are schools and churches. Politicians, of course, are known for it.

Examples:

Doctors: Probenecid may increase the levels of cephalosporins in the blood, since it may interfere with normal elimination.

Lawyers: It is agreed, during the term hereof, in good faith, that best endeavors will be employed, and advantages arising from the exploitation of rights assigned will be provided by the Articles of Association (which are hereby incorporated by reference), as now in force or as hereafter amended.

Military: The Peace Keeper is the necessary deterrent to war since it prevents the enemy from escalating its weapons stockpile.

The name "Peace Keeper," the MX Missile with multiple nuclear atomic warheads, is a perfect example of "doublespeak." This killing machine was named "Peace Keeper" by Ronald Reagan, the 39th President of the United States, because he — like thousands of other people — *believes* peace can come about only through a strong military defense. I think that the best way to bring about peace is to understand what causes conflict — in ourselves, in our families and friends, and people of other nations. Which of these two views is belief and which is fact? How can you find out?

How Do Propaganda and Double-talk Create Conflict?

There are many ways that confusing language can create conflict. Here are two examples of being lulled into a possibly dangerous situation:

Example:

Some kids you know at school think it would be fun to rob a local store owner, just for "kicks." These kids are super athletes and you admire them. They "double-talk" you into joining in and into believing that no one will get into trouble, and you believe them because they are "star" players. You decide to go along. The police show up and you are all arrested and put in jail.

Example:

The President gives a speech about the necessity of war with another country. The speech drones on for 60 minutes and double-talks about all the "wrongs" the other side has committed. By the time the speech ends, we are either (1) convinced the other country is at fault, or (2) asleep, and content to leave decisions to our leaders.

Activity #1: Make a List of Phrases

Keep a scrapbook of words used to distort the truth. Pay attention to TV ads, political speeches, religious sermons, school doctrines. Make a list of specific words and phrases called "Double-talk Samples." Ask your family and teachers to help you.

Activity #2: A Doublespeak Quiz

The following is a Military Doublespeak Quiz. See how many doublespeak phrases you can match up with their real meanings. (On a piece of paper, match the number on the left with a letter on the right.)

1.	Protective reaction strike	A.	Bullet hole
2.	Eliminate with extreme prejudice	B.	War Department
3.	Engage the enemy on all sides	C.	Poison the vegetation
4.	Tactical redeployment	D.	Bombs fell on target
5.	De-establish a government	E.	Atomic bomb
6.	Defense Department	F.	Atomic bomb
7.	Radiation enhancement device	G.	Bombing
8.	Defoliation	H.	Riot control
9.	Effective delivery	I.	Overthrow a government
10.	Predawn vertical insertion	J.	To ambush
11.	Strategic weapon	K.	Neutron bomb
12.	Tactical weapon	L.	Poisoning
13.	Confrontation management	M.	Invasion
14.	Resources control program	N.	Retreat
15.	Ballistically-induced aperture in the subcutaneous environment	O.	Kill

(See answers on page 52.)

Robot Thinking

Conditioning, as you already know, is a way to get you to think, speak and act in a particular way — out of habit, sort of like a robot. C3PO and R2D2 appeared as robots programmed to act and speak, in the movie "Star Wars." Someone pushed a button, and they regurgitated what they'd been taught.

There are times when you and I act like those robots. We've been programmed, or conditioned, to be "the good little girl," or "the obedient little boy." We do what we are told because our families or teachers have taught us to *believe* we should. This kind of conditioning, however, can keep us from knowing who we are. Double-talk and propaganda prevent us from knowing ourselves and each other. Peace comes from *understanding* each other and one another's conflict — not from being blind to it or pretending it's not there. A peaceful mind is a clear mind.

Activity:

Please write to me if you find any interesting doublespeak messages. I will share them with the young people in the school I am working at here in California. My address is at the back of this book.

If you need a break, this might be a good time for some exercise, a favorite radio program, or taking care of that project you were supposed to finish yesterday! While you're walking,

Answers to Doublespeak Quiz: (1 - G) (2 - O) (3 - J) (4 - N) (5 - I) (6 - B) (7 - K) (8 - C) (9 - D) (10 - M) (11 - E) (12 - F) (13 - H) (14 - L) (15 - A)

or working with your hands, take time to think about what you've read about in this chapter. Remind yourself that in any given situation, peaceful behavior can always be your first choice.

In the section that follows, we will read a story about two soldiers caught in a frightening battle. Then we will look at what happens inside all of us when we fall into the trap of war.

Sergeant Stone's Revenge
A Story

"Throw me my M-16 and grenade launcher," Sergeant Stone yelled to Dillon. "They're coming down the hill!"

The battle screams of the northern troops were terrifying, freezing our souls. Unable to move, Private Dillon stared blankly at the trees above, the foreign cries of death descending upon him. He heard his sergeant yelling at him from 20 feet away, but it sounded as if they were at opposite ends of a long, dark tunnel.

"Dillon! Wake up, you crazy fool!" Sergeant Stone was screaming. The sergeant had to duck a spray of bullets coming from an automatic rifle. Rolling quickly to his left, he came up against Dillon who was frozen in fear in a makeshift dugout shelter.

"Dillon! Where are you?"

He slapped Private Dillon once, then again and again.

Dillon suddenly returned to consciousness. "What are you doing? Where are we? What's happening? I don't belong here. Let me go!" He started to turn away from the hill, but Sergeant Stone stopped him.

"You coward! You can't run away! Your men depend on you. Your country depends on you. You've got to fight for your nation, for freedom, for democracy, for peace! You can't let your country down, Dillon. We've got to take this hill. The enemy is evil! They deserve to die!"

"Sarge, I can't do it! I'm scared! I don't wanna die." Dillon was crying.

"Shut up, you coward! You can't desert. You're a soldier! You must kill or die, or you dishonor our flag!"

The cries of the enemy were coming closer. The air was charged with deafening explosions. The enemy was launching its largest attack yet. Both sides were determined to take that hill. Neither side would back down. They had been there for almost 10 days, which seemed like a lifetime. Each side had heavy casualties. Human beings were killed in horrible ways — bombed, shot, bayonetted in close combat. The night fighting was a nightmare — crawling on their bellies inch by inch, in absolute terror, each moment facing death. Then suddenly there would be flares, and the hill was lit up like a night baseball game back home, with everything aglow in a strange play-like brilliance. It was unreal and, at the same time, all too real.

Any noise at night was enough to stiffen every muscle in their bodies. Reaching for their commando knives, they prodded ahead like giant bugs with feelers, sensing imminent danger, yet afraid to contact the soft flesh of the "enemy." They had been trained to override their instinct to pull back — and instead, to plunge their knives forward, then turn them to drive home their message.

"We didn't start the war, Dillon. They did!" Sergeant Stone

was shouting into Dillon's ear, and shaking him at the same time. "Get off your butt and get up that hill. Kill them and let God sort 'em out!"

"I can't move! My legs are frozen. I can't feel them." Dillon was frantically pulling at his legs.

"Get up! They're coming. You crazy idiot, come on. Be a hero. Take the hill. We've got to take it or they will get it! We can't let them get it again! We've got to get it back. You'll be decorated, Dillon. You'll get a medal if you can take the hill!" Sergeant Stone started firing his automatic rifle as he rose. "Come on, Dillon. It's time to meet the enemy or the devil. Take your choice!"

Sergeant Stone picked up Private Dillon by his gunbelt and hoisted him to his feet. He jammed his rifle into Dillon's hands and pushed him forward. Just then, the fighter jets went over for an assault on the hill, dropping fire bombs just a few hundred yards ahead of them. The sounds and sights were horrible. It was a living hell.

"Come on, Private. This is a gook hunting club and we are the star members! Kill 'em, kill 'em, kill 'em," Sergeant Stone screamed as he charged the hill.

There was a sudden explosion. Flying dirt, smoke and the stench of burning ground filled the air.

"Sarge! Sarge! Where are you? Sarge, I can't see you! Help me!" Dillon was calling out.

The Sergeant lay in a slump like a sack of potatoes in a hole, blown up by a land mine. Dillon turned away from that hole with a deep sickness in his being.

"It's my fault that he's dead!" cried Dillon. "I'm going to get them, for God and my country, and for Sergeant Stone, because

he is a real hero. He gave his life for his nation — for our cause, for freedom and peace. Now it's my turn. I'm not afraid any longer, Sarge. I'm coming, Sarge. Take this, you gooks!" Dillon rose up shouting. Charging, he threw a grenade at the advancing enemy troops that he could not see coming through the trees ahead of him.

This was a battle to end all battles. The hill was won. Only a few trees were left standing, and every living creature was destroyed, but the hill was "taken." It was part of the plan, the dream, the cause. We had to fight; we had to kill the enemy — for peace.

The movie ends. There are cheers in the audience. The military music plays loudly as the dead men's faces are re-shown on the screen. Hero: Private Jones. Hero: Corporal Smith. Hero: Private Dillon. Hero: Sergeant Stone. On and on go the names of the patriots who gave their lives for the flag, for their country — for peace.

The lights come up and you look around. The audience is slowly starting to rise and exit. Your heart is beating fast and your palms are sweaty. You feel angry, violent, ready to join the Armed Forces right now. You feel that if a "gook" were in the theater, you would attack him for what he did to those heroes on the screen. As you look around the theater at the other people in the audience, you see determined, angry looks and know that they're feeling what you're feeling. This movie has made you want to either (1) run away in fear and disgust, or (2) go to war.

Chapter 7

CREATING THE ENEMY

Enemy Images

People in military battles are trained to think of other people as enemies. The reason? The same reason we've seen all along: in order to survive. Soldiers know that if they meet up with "the other side" and are not prepared to kill, they may be killed themselves.

You and I don't fight military battles, but we sometimes become involved in other conflicts. If, for example, you are angry with me or afraid of me, and we happen to see each other on the street, before you ever approach me there is conflict going on between us — in your mind. Some inner cause in your brain has you blaming me for something that you think is my fault. Before we even speak, there is a war going on.

When our brain makes an "enemy" out of someone, it goes through certain patterns of thought that separate us from that person. The following are a few examples of enemy-making thoughts. Ask yourself, as you read them, if you have thought this way about anyone, or if you suspect anyone has thought this way about you. Don't judge yourself for having these thoughts — we've all had them. They're part of being human.

1. You are Different from Me.

We human beings have many differences between us. We vary in the color of our skins, the shape of our facial features, the way we walk and talk, the languages we speak, where we live, what we or our parents do for a living, where our family comes from, the clothes we wear. These differences make for variety in human culture, and they do not have to be conflict producing.

•Name three ways in which you are "different" from a person you know:

1. _____ .

2. _____ .

3. _____ .

•Have these differences kept you from getting along with this person? Do any of these differences make an "enemy" out of this person? How?

2. You are a Stranger.

As soon as we label a human being "a stranger," we create a separation between us. Cowboy movies always seem to have a line like, "There's a stranger in town. Who is he?" The stranger is treated as if he has the plague. By seeing a person as a "stranger," "foreigner" or "outsider," we present an attitude of "me vs. you." We create conflict before we've even met the person.

• Do you consider some people strangers? Who are they?

1. _____ .

2. _____ .

3. _____ .

• Why do you consider them "strangers"? Have you stopped to consider that these "strangers" may see *you* as a stranger? How would you feel if you were a new kid in town and everyone in school regarded you as a "stranger"?

3. You are a Bad Person.

Another way we create the "enemy" is to see someone as "bad." When we make someone "bad," we are blaming them. Some people have a need to make others look "bad" so they can look "good." Name someone you see as "bad." Why is she/he "bad"?

1. _____ .

2. _____ .

3. _____ .

4. You are The Devil in Disguise.

People at war make heavy use of this approach. They make their "enemies" inhuman or evil, because they find it easier to kill someone who is less than human. In the war movie, "Sergeant Stone's Revenge," the warrior called the other side "gooks." Calling them by this name made them seem worthless. If he had seen them as fellow *human* beings, he might have found it impossible to shoot them. That's how war works: we degrade and humiliate people in order to be able to kill them.

5. You are a Horrible Creature.

When we make other people seem like frightening, disgusting animals, we can then "step on them" and feel that we are right in doing so. We can more easily crush a spider, or shoot a rat, or stone a poisonous snake, or kill another human being if we see them as monsters that need to be "exterminated." We are able to kill people because we have been conditioned to see them as harmful creatures that are threatening our welfare.

Roleplaying
to Understand Differences

When we see differences between ourselves and others as reasons to be separate, we create conflict. When we see differences between ourselves and others as interesting, we can learn something new.

You have already learned that we grow up "conditioned" to have certain *beliefs*; people who live in other countries also grow up conditioned to have beliefs. When these beliefs differ, it creates conflict. The Arabs and Israelis prove this to us continuously.

People within the same country can also grow up with different beliefs and fight over them. In the mid-1800s, the United States was in such turmoil over slavery that the north fought the south in the U.S. Civil War. Households can have civil wars too. Beliefs can cause conflict between a father and mother, parents and children, sisters and brothers.

The following exercise is called "**roleplay**." Think about the questions: Why do we have beliefs? What purpose do they serve? Do beliefs separate people? Can we live without beliefs?

Put yourself in the shoes of someone else and play the part of that person — like actors do. When you roleplay, you find out what it feels like to be someone different. This can help you understand how another person thinks and feels.

You can do this roleplay alone or with another. If you do it alone, first put yourself in Dale's shoes; the second time you read it, put yourself in Jan's shoes. Let yourself get into the part you are reading. If you do the roleplay with another person, first play one part; then switch and play the other part.

Roleplay:

Dale: *(Angry)*   "You're the new kid, aren't you?"

Jan: *(Calm)*   "That's right. My name is Jan."

Dale: "What makes you think I want to know your name?"

Jan: "It's a common courtesy to tell your name when you first meet."

Dale: "Well, I don't want to know the name of a stranger."

Jan: "I hope I'm not a stranger for long."

Dale: "We don't think much of strangers around here. You should get out, move somewhere else."

Jan: "I like it here. I've met some friendly people."

Dale: "Well, you don't look like you belong here."

Jan: "Sorry about that. I didn't think people had to look like they belonged anywhere in particular. Aren't you Dale?"

Dale: "Never mind who I am. I hear you're hot stuff. You think you know it all because you know Karate. Let's see what you've got."

Jan: "Look, I don't want to fight. I'm not a fighter and, besides, you're bigger than I am. Can't we be friends?"

Dale: "Strangers make us look bad. And one stranger even robbed us. You strangers think you can come here and take over."

Jan: "I don't want to take over. Come on, let's shake hands.

Dale: *(Slaps Jan's hand away)* "I don't shake with strangers." *(Walks away)*

Questions:

Think a moment about how you felt playing your role:

1. Did you get angry?
2. Were you afraid? If so, of what?
3. Did you offer a reward for doing things your way?
4. Did you offer punishment? Did you blame?
5. Did you hide any thoughts or feelings? Which ones?
6. Did you see the other person as "The Enemy"?
7. Were you working to be "A Hero"?
8. Was there any point where you felt you ought to either fight or run away?
9. How did you feel being Dale? Jan?

Chapter 8

HOW WE HANDLE VIOLENCE

You know that we humans have been fighting to survive for as long as we can remember. We've been conditioned to have certain beliefs, and many of these beliefs cause conflict — in our minds and in the world. We've learned to face a conflict situation by either fighting or running away. We've been taught to be "good" and to "win."

The Problem with "Good"

There are major problems that arise when we aim to be "good":

1. It's hard to be "good" when there are so many different opinions about what "good" is. (Rambo's idea of "good" is to fight violence with violence; a Karate Master's idea of good is to prevent violence before it begins.)

2. If we set up a standard of what "good" is and try to live by that standard, we create conflict within ourselves. (My father's idea of "good" is finishing all the food on my plate. If I eat any more, I'll get a stomach ache.)

3. Being a "good girl" or "good boy" can mean spending a lot of time focusing on all the things you're *not* supposed to do. (My mother's idea of "good" is not eating snacks

before dinner, not staying out too late, and not forgetting to mow the lawn.)

4. Because we want to be "good," we don't want to accept behavior in ourselves that we see as "bad." As a result, we hide such behavior or blame it on someone else by "escape" thinking. ("It's Dana's fault that we lost the game.")

5. Being "good" and doing only what we are told as children can lead us to grow into adults who never question what we are told. We learn to leave decisions up to "the experts" — those who supposedly know more than we do. This can be dangerous. Many "experts" are not as knowledgeable as they seem. Some "experts" are ill-intentioned; they use double-talk and propaganda to get us to do what they want.

When we work hard to be "good," we sometimes get so caught up in what we're *not* supposed to do, we forget to think positively — about what we *are* supposed to do, what we *want* to do, *need* to do, *love* to do. We doubt our own feelings and become afraid to tell anyone how we feel; we fear we might be bad or wrong, or that someone will tell us *not* to feel that way. We feel inner conflict, and we don't know how to resolve it.

Inner Conflict Can Create Violence

We often hear someone say, "Don't be like *them*. Be like *us*." War protesters do this. But, as you already know, if there's going to be a group called "them" and a group called

66

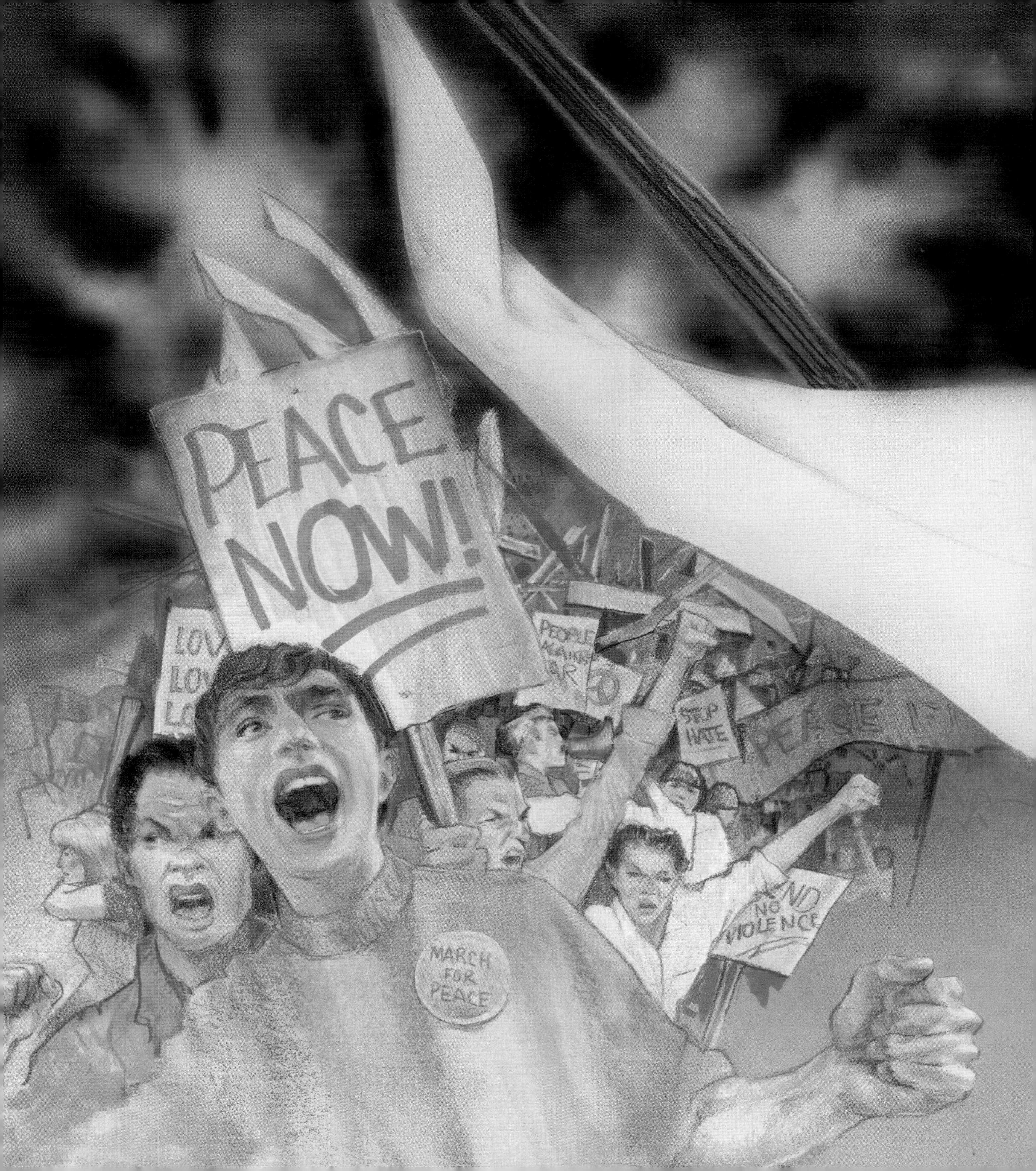
PEACE NOW!
STOP HATE
MARCH FOR PEACE
NO VIOLENCE

"us," the tug of war is going to continue, and we're not going to get any closer to understanding our conflict.

You may have noticed that many students are competing in school for good grades, and they'll be competing for high-paying jobs when they're out in the world. This competitive way of life means that in order to succeed, we have to defeat the other side. Who can get better grades? The finest clothes? The fastest car?

Inside yourself, you may feel confused and frustrated — and sometimes angry and violent. You feel as if the whole world is a battlefield. You want to be a "good" citizen, but you feel that the country you live in is pushing you to compete for things you're not sure you want, for reasons you're not sure you agree with.

One of your inner conflicts is:
"I don't want to let my angry and violent feelings out,
but holding them inside doesn't feel good either."

If *you* have violent, warlike feelings inside of you, and you know a friend or two with violent, warlike feelings inside of them, there must be hundreds of thousands of people who have violent feelings too. It suddenly may become clear to you how people get into disagreements, misunderstandings and, finally, major war. We are a world of people who are running, fighting and competing — one against the other — person against person, nation against nation — "we" vs. "them" — in a violent struggle for survival.

68

Questions:

    1. Do you ever have violent feelings?
    2. If so, what kind?
    3. How do you deal with them?

Talking and thinking about conflict can make us feel unsettled, but it's important to keep on talking and thinking because that's the best way to reach understanding.

Activity:

Take some time to write down a list of "Things That Make Me Feel Violent." Ask a friend or one of your parents or brothers or sisters to make a list too. Compare them. Do your lists agree? Do they disagree? Do you have a lot in common?

Remember:
We are what we think.

Fighting Fire with Fire

Let's suppose a boy named John accused you of being stupid and never doing anything right. He said *words* that triggered hurt or violent feelings inside you. Every time you see John, your *memory* reminds you of his words, and the violent feelings return.

Perhaps you want to hit John, yell at him, or hurt him back. How would you handle these feelings? Would you ignore him? Would you go ahead and hit him? Shout some nasty words at him? Tease him?

If you acted on your feelings and hit John, you would get some of your violent feelings out of your system, but there is a good chance that you would not feel satisfied. The hurt feelings would still be inside you, unresolved. This is a case of fighting fire with fire just making more fire.

On the other hand, if you never acted on your feelings, there's a good chance you would be frustrated, being unable to express how you feel.

The following two approaches — fighting and being "heroic" — are presented so that you can put yourself into the situation as you read, and think about how you would feel taking these approaches.

Approach #1: Be violent.

A. Your inner voice is saying, "John is a first-class idiot. I hate him and I'd like to tear his insides out. I'd like to see him get run over by a car, or attacked by an alien from outer space. I wish he would dry up and die."

B. Every time you see John, you fume inside. The fire gets hotter and hotter. Since you see him every day, your feelings of conflict build, until finally one day you can stand it no longer. You walk up to John, and you say, "Listen, you idiot, you deserve this." And you punch him.

Okay. You've got your violent feelings out. What happens now?

1. Do you feel better?
2. Do you think John will call you names again?

3. How will you feel if he does?

4. Have you resolved your conflict?

Approach #2: Be heroic.

Here's another way your brain may handle this situation.

A. You recognize that the feeling you have is violent. You hear your inner voice: "My heart is beating fast; my fists are clenched; I am ready to explode. This feeling is violent!"

B. Your brain judges that feeling. It says, "That's a *bad* feeling. It's *wrong* to feel this. I am bad if I feel this feeling." As a result, you feel guilty.

C. Your brain compares your violent feeling to a nonviolent feeling and starts giving you commands: "I *should not* feel violent; violence is *bad*. I *should* feel nonviolent; nonviolence is *good*."

D. Your brain creates "The Hero," the "Ideal Person," to represent the image of goodness you *should* be. You ask yourself what a hero would do. You decide that a hero would "turn the other cheek" (not take any violent action).

So, you turn the other cheek, even though you are still fuming. Your brain has talked you into being the good guy, because you have been *conditioned* to be a "good person." That voice in your conscience says, okay, now you're being "good" —

71

but you are feeling upset, angry and frustrated. What you feel is conflict.

So, you've managed to control your actions. What happens now?

1. Do you feel better?
2. Do you think John will call you names again?
3. How will you feel if he does?
4. Have you resolved your conflict?

Cooling the Fire with Water

There is a third approach that you may never have tried before. Rather than fighting fire with fire, you cool it down with water. Instead of focusing on John, your "enemy," you *look* at your thoughts and feelings and *accept* them.

Approach #3: Understand Yourself.

A. You recognize that the feeling you have is violent. You hear your inner voice: "My heart is beating fast; my fists are clenched; I am ready to explode. **"This is a violent feeling!"**

B. You *look* at the violent feeling. You do not judge it as "good" or "bad." You don't try to make it go away. You *look* at it and recognize that it's a feeling you have. You say: **"This is a feeling I have."** Say it to yourself.

C. Let the feeling be there. Say: **"It's okay for this feeling to be inside me."** Once you make it okay to be inside you, you acknowledge that you sometimes have violent feelings. We all do.

D. Ask yourself why you think the feeling is there. Attempt to understand it. **This feeling is inside me, because**

_____ .

E. Remind yourself that your *mind* put that feeling there.

Okay. You've acknowledged your feeling. What happens now?

1. Do you feel better?
2. Do you think John will call you names again?
3. How will you feel if he does?
4. Have you resolved your conflict?

Questions:

1. Have you ever looked at your angry or violent feelings in this way before — *just* looking at them, accepting them as okay?
2. How is this way different from the way you usually see your feelings?
3. What happens to your violent feelings when you just look at them?
4. If your brain created your violent feelings, do you think you could replace the violent feelings in your mind? How?

Understanding this may take time. If you don't understand it yet, don't worry! The more time you take to learn
about conflict and understand yourself, the easier it will get.

Congratulations! You've come a long way in understanding
conflict in yourself and others. Take a break if you need one,
because the following story is the scariest of all — and it really
happened, not exactly this way, but it happened.

GOD'S FLASH PHOTO OF EARTH
A Story

As you walk to school, you are aware of the birds chirping,
the warm sun on the rich green leaves of the trees, and the
fresh cut grass smell of spring in the air. Flowers are bursting
into pink, yellow, red and lavender, and the clear blue sky is
dotted with beautiful white clouds. The cool breeze makes you
feel peaceful and fills you with a sense of wonder.

You walk into your classroom, greet your classmates and
take a seat. The teacher announces that you are going to see a
movie. Your eyes move from the soft colors of spring outside the
classroom window to the light of the screen in front of you.

You are instantly drawn to the family you see in their home
eating breakfast. They are getting ready to go to school and to
work. Now they are getting into the car. Their neighborhood
looks very much like yours.

Like an invisible observer, you are in the car with them.
As you tune into their words, you hear anxious talk about the
future. The news comes on the radio. You pass by televisions
in store windows with groups of people watching. Every

program has been interrupted by a special announcement.

"War! The enemy has declared war!" One of our nuclear destroyers, while off the enemy's coast, fired on two of their bombers, exploding a nuclear warhead on one of the planes — we report, in defense. The explosion was so great that it was felt for hundreds of miles. Everything was destroyed in the immediate area, including the ship, the planes, and small fishing villages along the coast.

Thousands of people are filling the hospitals, and thousands of others are fleeing the fallout. Right now, the Ninth Fleet is preparing to go into action. Our Defense Secretary has issued a "red alert" sending all Armed Forces into immediate preparedness.

The news broadcast says our Embassy has been captured and our Ambassador and staff have been imprisoned. In the last two days since the atomic explosion, one of our bases has been bombed, as well as one of our ships off their coast. Many soldiers and sailors have been killed and wounded.

Leaders of the two countries are arguing with each other. One says it was an accident; the other says it was a deliberate attack. The emergency talks are not going well. Everyone is angry and afraid. They say we are the enemy, because we invented the atomic bomb and used it against innocent men, women and children. We say they are the enemy because they attacked first, and we had to defend ourselves.

As this family listens to their car radio, you continue to hear constant up-to-the-minute broadcasts of the events. There was another attack on American soldiers last night. The President is calling for a Total Five-Star Alert. We are preparing for the worst. All talks between the two nations have

stopped, and there is a dead calm in the air, as if a storm were brewing.

The faces of this family are lined with tension as they drive to school and to work, trying to proceed as if it were another normal day. They drive by the Military Air Force Command Station, which was built eight years ago under strict secrecy. No one knows what's on this base, but people suspect nuclear missiles. Strong, serious soldiers stand before the barbed wire fence. Nearby, there is a field where fighter planes land. During the last several days there has been more activity than usual. Jeeps with important looking officials have been seen going in, but not coming out. Rumors are that this station has a Nuclear Survival City dug many feet below the surface to house top government, military and business leaders, should there ever be a nuclear attack.

The car turns onto the main road of their town, a small suburb of New Metro, one of the largest and most successful cities in the country. New Metro has a huge financial center and is noted for its far-reaching computer network. Many companies situated here make weapons and war systems for the military. Because of booming business, many families have been attracted to the area.

New Metro, at one time, was rolling farmland with small grassy hills as far as the eye could see. Cows used to graze there and, in the spring, bright mustard plants grew wild, covering the fields in a blanket of yellow. Now there are rows of concrete, windowless buildings, paved roads and neon lit shopping malls.

As the car drives along Route 10 toward the school, everything seems to be dead still, as if even the birds are stopped in flight, as if the wind has ceased blowing, and every single living thing is frozen in an instant of time. The sky suddenly fills with a light so bright that their eyes are blinded. For a moment that seems like forever, they are caught in this gigantic explosion of light, as if God has taken a flash photo of earth from heaven. And just as lightning is followed by thunder, a deafening blast follows the flash, like hundreds of thousands of airplanes breaking through the sound barrier — or like the monstrous roar of a million cannons. Then, a deadness and darkness descends.

Cars swerve to the side of the road, some running into each other. This family's car pulls over, banging into the guard rail. Faces are frozen, eyes temporarily blinded, and in the distance a mountainous smoking thundercloud is speeding upward into space.

"Oh, my God! We've done it!" someone cries. And then the endless fire begins.

All of a sudden the light stops flickering and you gradually become aware of the classroom. Outside the window the sunlight is still dancing on new green leaves, birds are singing, and the moment is peaceful once again. The silence is broken by your teacher's voice.

"Students, I hope this movie didn't frighten you too much. I've shown it to you so that you can begin to understand that something like this could happen, as it did in Japan during World War II when the United States dropped atomic bombs on Hiroshima and Nagasaki."

You try to look unshaken, but the truth is that you are anxious and upset by this movie — mainly because it wasn't just another movie. It was about something that really happened, not many years ago — and it could easily happen

79

again. You look out the window to recapture the feeling of peace and calm you had while walking to school.

Your first reaction? Probably it's either to leave the room and forget you ever saw this movie (run), or to rage at people who are responsible for making and dropping bombs (fight). You realize that countries like Russia and the United States have the ability to drop bombs that could totally wipe out civilization.

Perhaps your teachers have presented ideas for peace to you and your classmates. Or perhaps your class has written to school children in Russia about war. Russian people don't want war either, but they are afraid that our government will use the atomic bomb on them. They see our country as a possible *enemy*, and a powerful one.

Questions:

1. Have you ever thought that the United States might be an "enemy" to other people? Does this thought shock you?
2. Do you think of your country as the hero, fighting for freedom?
3. What would make the United States an enemy to another country?
4. Do you think the United States has been afraid of other countries? Which ones?
5. Do you think other countries have been afraid of the United States? Which ones?
6. How could we reach the point in a disagreement that would cause us to explode an atomic bomb — and kill thousands of people?

Chapter 9

A NEW WAY TO HANDLE VIOLENCE

This story was written by a man named Chuang Tzu (Ch-wong-Zoo) in China many years ago:

There was a man who was so disturbed by the sight of his own shadow and so displeased with his own footsteps that he made up his mind to get rid of both. The method he came up with was to run away from them.

So, he got up and ran. But every time he put his foot down, there was another step. And his shadow kept up with him without the slightest difficulty. He thought that perhaps he was not running fast enough. So, he ran faster and faster, without stopping, until he finally dropped dead. He failed to realize that if he merely stepped into the shade, his shadow would vanish. And if he stopped moving and sat down, there would be no more footsteps.

Are You Your Own Enemy?

People have been trying to run away from their shadows for thousands of years. The reason we have difficulty running away from our shadows is that our shadows are part of us. And there's no way we can run away from ourselves, no matter how fast we run, or how far we go. That's why we need to accept ourselves — shadows and all. Anything else creates inner conflict.

In the same way that your mind envisions someone else as a "bad guy" or "the enemy," your view of yourself also begins in your mind. So, if you see yourself as "bad," your mind has made an enemy out of you.

Have there been times when you've made an enemy out of yourself in your own mind? Have you said or done something that has caused you to think badly of yourself? If so, you're not alone; we all do that. We human beings are not perfect, and there will always be times when we "make mistakes."

The healthiest way to handle these times is to *look* at your thoughts instead of judging them as "bad." Feeling guilty about something you said or did will not change what happened in the past. Like athletes who lose a game, all you can do is look at what happened, *learn* from it, and keep going. Holding guilty feelings inside does not make you feel good and does not help you (or anyone).

Facing Your Shadow

The part of you that you judge as "bad" is like a "shadow." The more "bad" you think you are, the more scary and painful the shadow becomes. And the more scary and painful it becomes, the less you want to come face-to-face with it. The shadow lives in your mind like a frightening creature waiting to invade your nightmares.

Perhaps some thoughts have been so frightening or hurtful that you've decided to hide them, or project them onto someone else (the enemy, "them"). Your brain forgets that this "shadow" began in your own mind, with your own thought or feeling.

It is you! Judging these thoughts/feelings (as bad) caused a division in yourself, as the *judger* (the person who wants to change) and the *judged* (those thoughts/feelings that are bad). This division is at the root of conflict in yourself and in all humans. It is a basic cause of conflict inwardly. This judgment creates a shadow inside and then this shadow gets "projected" outside as the enemy, the bad guy, the devil. We only want to see ourselves as the hero or good guy (on the side of God). This creates tremendous conflict — inwardly and outwardly.

Inwardly, we are divided between being bad (the should not, but who we actually are) and having to be good (the should, or who we think we ought to be: our ideal, our hero, our Godlike image of goodness). Outwardly we see *our*selves (*our* group, nation, political party, religion, culture) as the "Freedom Fighters," the heroes — as opposed to the "Terrorists," the villains. We are divided inwardly and outwardly. This division shows up in identifying with (wanting to be like) other people like ourselves, which creates nationalism (boundaries that create conflict) or racism (differences that create conflict). These divisions lead to competition — each group, nation, sect trying to outdo the other, each divided and in conflict, each clinging to beliefs that separate human beings.

Inward Conflict
Creates Outward Conflict

If we can see that judgment creates fundamental division within ourselves, we will be able to understand conflict at its root and end it there. This is the most important thing this book is saying! Once there is self-judgment, the war is on. The seeds have been sown.

The Root of Conflict
Comes from Self-Judgment

Is this a belief or a fact? How will you find out?

Let's look at the creation of the "shadow" (the judged thoughts/feelings) and how to deal with that. We will use a simple example to show you how and where it starts. From this small beginning, can you see how global conflict might be created? Here's a way to deal with your shadows.

Healing the Division in Your Brain

1. Don't Judge Your Thoughts.

The first rule in healing the division in your brain between good and evil is to refrain from judging your thoughts as "good" or "bad." Some of your thoughts are going to be positive, and some are going to be negative. That's just part of being a human being.

Example: I hate Susan.

2. Watch Your Thoughts.

Look at your thoughts without trying to change them in any way. This is called "**observing**." It's different from learning mathematics or a new language. Instead of busying your brain with how, where, why or what — you just stop, look at your thoughts, listen to them and become AWARE of them.

Example: I hate Susan.

This is a thought and feeling I have.

Being a good listener/observer will help you, no matter what you do or where you go. This comes from merely being aware each moment to what is happening around you and inside you. It is becoming aware of how you are thinking and feeling.

Example:

Let the thought/feeling about Susan just be there. Tell yourself that it's all right. Just watch. Don't try to do anything about it. Try to see what is behind the hate. Did it begin with self-hate, self-judgment? Does outward judgment and hate start with inward judgment and hate? Why do we judge ourselves? What purpose does it serve? What does it actually create?

Watch and listen to your thoughts and feelings for a few minutes each day, or whenever you have the time. You can do it anywhere once you get used to it: on the bus, while exercising or waiting for your dinner to cook — any free moment is an opportunity to observe thinking. The idea is not to *stop* thinking, but to *watch* thinking, to be aware of how thinking judges behavior in order to change it and, in so doing, creates conflict.

There are very good reasons for your thoughts and feelings. Sometimes they are symptoms of inner conflict. Once you *observe* them, accept them as yours, and *think* about them, you begin to recognize the causes of your inner conflict, and you can learn to resolve it.

This kind of observation will help you develop **"insight"**: the ability to *see* what's going on inside yourself. In the process, you will become *aware* of what's going on inside other people as well. This will help you *face conflict* and its fundamental causes so you can end it at its root.

Accept Yourself

There are millions of people who see themselves as "not good" or "not good enough." They've been *conditioned* to see themselves this way, either by their surroundings or by the people in their lives. If you are one of these people, there is something you can do. You can begin to accept yourself for who you are. Accepting yourself exactly as you are creates peace of mind and makes you more accepting of others for who they are. You and I are not villains, and we are not heroes. We are human beings. The process for accepting yourself is to simply do it. Start, right here and right now. "I accept myself. I am what I am. What I am is neither bad nor good. It is just a fact. Judging myself in order to change what I am only creates conflict. Seeing myself for what I actually am deepens my understanding."

**We can always change and improve ourselves,
but we must begin by accepting the person we are.
Acceptance leads to understanding.
Understanding leads to freedom.**

Activity:

Here are more ways to "practice" knowing yourself and others around you.

1. Find a friend or family member who would like to practice with you.
2. Choose a violent thought or feeling that you have had. It can be real or one that you've made up.
3. Roleplay yourself or someone who feels violent. Go through the process of healing the division in your brain.
4. Watch your thoughts and feelings without judging them.
5. Add to your list of "Thoughts That Cause Conflict."

**When we can share how we create conflict,
and admit our conflict-making thoughts to one another,
we will have a basis for working together to end conflict.**

Shadows That Come Out At Night

As you have learned, your violent thoughts and feelings can get buried inside you where you can't see them. They can be hidden in your unconscious or subconscious thoughts. Sometimes these thoughts and feelings appear in your dreams. Dreams can be exciting, but they can also be confusing and frightening. Some are powerful — so much so that when you wake up you sometimes still feel the emotions of the dream.

But dreams are only thoughts you create, like making a movie in your mind. You can watch your thoughts as if you were in a theater, part of an audience watching a movie on a screen. Remember that there is nothing to do but *watch*. If

your violent thoughts and feelings come to the surface where you can see them, don't worry — this is a healthy thing! Whether you watch your thoughts during the day or at night in your dreams, it's good to let them come up. This gives you the opportunity to find out that you don't have to be afraid of them. When they do come up, look at them and accept them *without* trying to do anything about them.

When you allow your most frightening thoughts and feelings to come to the surface, where you can watch them and talk about them, it's like opening the doors and windows of a house full of bats. You open up and watch them fly out. Once you let them go, you feel freer.

Remember:
Peace is always in us.
Only *we* prevent it from happening.

Chapter 10

PRACTICING UNDERSTANDING

If you play a musical instrument, draw or paint, write or take photographs, participate in sports or the Martial Arts, you know that practice makes perfect — or at least closer to as perfect as we humans can get! The same is true for understanding ourselves and others.

If you are looking for ways to help you fine-tune your understanding, I suggest the following exercises and activities. These exercises will probably be most meaningful if they're done with friends and family members. Perhaps your teacher will allow you to bring them to class so that your classmates can participate. However you do them, alone or with others, I hope they help you reach a higher level of understanding, and I hope you have fun with them.

Talk About Fear and Anger

Whenever you feel it will help you, talk about your fear and anger, and help others by listening to them talk about theirs.

Exercise #1:

1. Name a fear that you have.
2. Can you think of any actions you've taken as a result of this fear? What are they?

3. Can you recall thoughts you had before you took those actions? What were they?
4. Can you see how your fear is causing you conflict?

Exercise #2:

1. What was the last thing that made you very angry?
2. What action(s) did you take because of your anger?
3. Do you remember the thoughts you had that caused you to take those actions? What were they?
4. Can you see how your anger caused *you* conflict?
5. Can you think of some way you could resolve your angry feelings?

The World Language Game

This game will help lessen any fear you may have about "foreign" and/or "strange" people.

1. Find a book that has foreign phrases in it. Some of the easier language books to find will be Spanish, Japanese, Russian, French and German. If there are any simple ones from the Middle East or Africa that provide English pronunciations, use those too.

2. Learn some simple phrases or greetings, such as:
English: Good day! (Hello. Hi. Greetings.)
Spanish: Buenos días!
Japanese: Ohayō gozaimasu
Russian: Dobree dyen

French: Bonjour
German: Guten Tag

3. Learn to say simple things, such as:
   What food is this?
   Where is the train station?
   Thank you very much.
   Please, may I?

Take turns playing different parts. Greet each other in one language and respond in the same language.

Example in Spanish:

Person No. 1: Buenos días! Cómo está?
              (Good day! How are you?)

Person No. 2: Muy bien, gracias. ¿Y usted?
              (Fine, thanks. And you?)

By using foreign languages, fear of the "foreigner" diminishes and you discover that foreigners are only "other people." Spoken language is really nothing more than convenient noises — a process of vocal cords, lips, tongue and breath working together. Look at the written word "scary." It's merely a scribble of blue or black fluid on paper! Language comes from an image created in our brains that translates into a word, picture or sound — so we can communicate.

We can't learn all the languages in the world, but if we make the effort to learn some phrases, to reach out and communicate with "foreigners," they won't be strangers any more.

Is It a Fact or Is It a Belief?

This game can be played with two or more people. Let one person make a statement, such as "The world is round." Go around the room and ask:

A. Is this statement a fact or a belief?

B. If the answer is, "It's a fact," ask:
    (1) How do you know it's a fact?
    (2) Describe your proof.

C. If the answer is, "It's a belief," ask:
    (1) Do you believe this? If the answer is yes, ask:
        (a) *Why* do you believe this?
        (b) Is what you believe *true*?
    (2) If the answer is no, ask:
        (a) Why don't you believe this?
        (b) How do you know, or why do you feel, it's not true?

Here are some sample statements you might want to try:

"In order to have peace, we must fight."
"We need weapons and Armed Forces to achieve peace."
"Conflict can only be solved by experts."
"To have peace, we should act peacefully."
"In order to be nonviolent, we must act nonviolently."
"The way to end conflict is through understanding conflict."
"Understanding conflict can bring about peace."

"Understanding the causes of war can end war."
"Understanding what prevents peace is understanding what creates war."
"The root of war is within us, in the way we think and act."

What Do You Think About Conflict?

The following questions can be helpful in understanding what creates conflict. These questions can be used to open your mind, to look at what you feel in your heart. Too often we listen to the voices of other people telling us how to think. Questioning helps you decide if you want to think those thoughts and act in those ways. Questioning helps to free your mind — a mind that is representative of the mind of all human beings — of destructive habits.

Discuss these questions with friends and family. Take them to school, and ask your teacher if you can have a group discussion about them — perhaps in your history class or "homeroom."

Ask your school to designate an "Understanding Conflict" day or night where parents, teachers and students participate in a discussion of these questions. Remember, there are no "right" or "wrong" answers.

The idea is to find out what you think and to offer reasons why you think the way you do. When we offer reasons for the way we think, people are better able to understand us.

1. Do you think that people can bring about peace through military strength?
2. How does society prepare us for war? In what ways? Where? At school? At home? On TV?
3. What effect do war toys, comics, videos or movies have on you?
4. What would happen to you if you refused to go to war?
5. What do your parents, teachers or friends tell you about war?
6. What effect do their opinions have on you?
7. Do you believe there are nonviolent alternatives to war? What are they?
8. Do you think that only political and military leaders cause war?
9. What responsibility do *you* have for war?
10. Do you think violent competition (cutthroat business) is like war? In what way?
11. Are there vocations that are not violent? Can you think of any vocations that are not competitive?
12. Do you see war as separate from your everyday life?
13. What are the things that make you feel violent?
14. What are some healthy ways in which you can handle your violent feelings?
15. What are some unhealthy ways?
16. Do other people's thoughts and feelings affect you? How?
17. Do you think your thoughts and feelings affect people around you?
18. Where does war start?
19. What does self-judgment have to do with war?
20. Can we understand the roots of conflict and end it?

A SPECIAL NOTE TO THE YOUNG READER

There are people who live their whole lives looking in only one direction, seeing things in a limited way. The wider your perspective, the more you see and the better you will be able to understand yourself, as well as other people. That's why I've written this book — to help you see other directions. Thank you for taking the time to read it.

There is more to understanding conflict than what is in this book. My purpose in writing it is to get you started. If you have any questions or comments about what you have read, ask your teachers, parents, or an older brother or sister to discuss it with you. You can also write to me if you wish. I would very much like to hear from you; it's a great pleasure for me to read letters from people who read my books. I'd also like to know if you enjoy the activities.

You can write to me as follows:

Terrence Webster-Doyle
Atrium Publications
P. O. Box 938
Ojai, California 93023

I hope to hear from you.

Affectionately,

Terrence Webster-Doyle

Terrence Webster-Doyle

P.S. Do you think a Martial Art like Karate can help us to solve conflict peacefully? Let's talk about it!

A Message to Parents, Teachers, Counselors or Anyone Who Works or Lives with Young People

No matter how noble the Utopian intention, trying to *bring about* peace only creates more conflict. It sounds strange, but it's true. Think of the countries at war today and how long they've been trying to work toward peace. The very means by which we think we will attain peace is the very means that is creating disorder and conflict.

This is not a book about "how to" get peace. **The intent of this book is to help young people understand peace by understanding the *causes* of conflict.** This may sound like a contradiction, but the difference is essential. Understanding leads to peace.

Life can be incredibly violent. Young people today face a world of tremendous pressure. Our daily relationships are based on competition — one person pitted against another person in an aggressive battle for survival of the self. We are, however, also in a period providing many opportunities for increasing our understanding and compassion. Most humans truly want cooperation rather than violence, and some doors are beginning to open.

Traditionally, the approach to peace has been through trying to live according to some philosophical, religious or political ideal. The logic has been simple and straightforward:

We are violent.
We must not be violent.
We should be peaceful.

In order to be peaceful,
we must get rid of our violence
and act nonviolently.

This type of "I *should* be peaceful — I *should not be* violent" thinking is one of the basic ways the mind tries to create order. In attempting to create order, however, we are thrown into deep conflict over what we should or should not do. And this is the problem.

101

There are many groups of people who are working toward bringing about world peace. Some of them use this should/should not kind of thinking. Some see the world as it is; others see it as they want it to be. Consider them:

The New Age Romantics. This group works to bring about world peace by "visualizing" it. They believe that in order to have a wonderful world, we have to imagine one. They visualize a world different from the one we have, and see that we do not have to accept what exists now. The "visualizing" creates the ideal, the Utopia, the "should," and hence more conflict between what is and what ought to be.

The "We are One" Proclaimers. These people proclaim that we are already one, and that the only thing standing in the way of world peace is the inability to see the simple truth of our "real" nature. The fact, however, is that right now in the world we are *not* one. We are divided, fragmented human beings. All else is theoretical and therefore illusory.

The Radical Activists. These intelligent, well-meaning people advocate getting involved in politics and protesting war, hunger, pollution and all the social ills of mankind. Their actions are fragmented and limited, but they do see that we have created our social problems and that we, therefore, are the ones who can end them. But this is not getting to the *root* of the problem.

The Violent Revolutionaries. These people are also concerned with ending war, pollution and hunger, but they believe that the only way to a solution is through revolution. They believe this so strongly that they will sometimes die or kill others for a cause. These people are often disillusioned with life, or they are so oppressed and mistreated that they see few other alternatives for getting what they want or need. This approach only begets more violence.

The Intellectuals. They ponder the problems of war. They read, write books, lecture to millions of people, and receive awards and degrees for their thoughts. Their ideals are lofty; their words mystify and inspire. They present "solutions" to the problems of humanity, and express them in clever ways. They mean well, but they have not been able to stop war. They are like the "visualizers," but are more sophisticated and educated.

Alternative Communities. In pursuit of an illusive life of peace, many people have joined "alternative" communities. They have dropped out of the "norm" to create new societies. They change their names, i.e., from John Smith to Running Bear Black Water, and shed their shopping mall clothing for sandals and a sarong. This is an understandable reaction to the horrors of a violent world, but often does not go beyond personal escape.

The Experts. Many of us, caught up in our day-to-day problems, have turned over the matter of world peace to "the experts" — educators, politicians, economists, psychologists, sociologists, religious leaders, anthropologists, historians. But understanding oneself and one's conflict is not a matter of expertise or specialty.

Peace can only be approached by a question — not an answer. It cannot be approached by an ideal or Utopian plan. Utopian plans, no matter how noble, create conflict because they are based on how we think life *should* be.

In order to bring about peace, we need to understand what is *not* peace; we need to look at what *prevents* peace. What prevents peace is *conflict* — conflict in our minds, in our thinking, and in our actions — and conflict is often exacerbated in trying to solve the problems conflict creates. We have either been shying away from our conflicts or fighting over them — not looking at them directly, face-to-face, without judgment or condemnation.

When we deny, condemn or run away from who and what we are (violent beings), and conform to what we should or would like to be (nonviolent beings), we only create more conflict.

Our work towards peace has failed because we continue to think of how to *solve the problem* of peace — how to *fix* it and *make* it work. In order to understand why there is conflict between us, we must ask:

1. Where does this division come from?
2. What is the root of this violence in ourselves?
3. What causes a person to call me his enemy?
4. What can we do together to understand the conflict between us?

There are those who believe that this subject matter is much too complicated — that if adults cannot deal with these issues, how can we expect young people to deal with them? I believe young people have a good chance of understanding what it means to live peacefully because they haven't yet become entrenched in the complexity of violence or of trying to be peaceful. They also tend to be more open to looking at something new than we over-educated adults who have experienced many unsuccessful attempts to put an end to conflict and war.

This book is intended to awaken young people to the nature and structure of conflict, violence. To help them understand the concepts in this book, I would recommend that you read and discuss it with them. I ask only that they *look, question, and find out for themselves* if what is being said is true. You can help them most by making the discovery enjoyable. This is the most significant aspect of educating our children — giving them the gift of understanding themselves in relationship.

ABOUT THE AUTHOR

Terrence Webster-Doyle was Founder and Director of three independent schools and has taught at the secondary, community college and university levels in Education, Psychology and Philosophy. He has worked in Juvenile Delinquency Prevention and has developed counseling programs for teenagers. He has earned a doctorate degree in Psychology, has produced numerous conferences and workshops on New Directions in Education, and was the Director of The Center for Educational Alternatives in Northern California. Currently, he is Co-director of a secondary school whose intent is to explore psychological conditioning, and is working on a series of children's books exploring this theme.

Books for young people by Terrence Webster-Doyle:

Facing the Double-Edged Sword:
The Art of Karate for Young People*

Fighting the Invisible Enemy:
The Effects of Conditioning on Young People

Why is Everybody Always Picking on Me?:
A Guide to Handling Bullies for Young People

Books for adults by Terrence Webster-Doyle:

Growing Up Sane: *Understanding the Conditioned Mind*

Brave New Child: *Education for the 21st Century*

The Religious Impulse: *A Quest for Innocence*

Peace — The Enemy of Freedom: *The Myth of Nonviolence*

Karate: *The Art of Empty Self*

One Encounter, One Chance: *The Essence of Take Nami Do Karate***

*Finalist: Benjamin Franklin Award • Winner: Award of Excellence, Ventura Ad Society
**Finalist, Benjamin Franklin Award — Psychology/Self-Help

ABOUT THE PUBLISHER

Atrium Publications concerns itself with fundamental issues which prevent understanding and cooperation in human affairs. Starting with the fact that our minds are conditioned by our origin of birth, our education and our experiences, Atrium Publications' intent is to bring this issue of conditioning to the forefront of our awareness. Observation of the fact of conditioning — becoming directly aware of the movement of thought and action — brings us face-to-face with the actuality of ourselves. Seeing who we actually are, not merely what we think we are, reveals the potential for a transformation of our ways of being and relating.

If you would like more information, please write or call us. Again, we enjoy hearing from people who read our books and we appreciate your comments.

Atrium Publications
P. O. Box 938
Ojai, California 93023
(805) 646-0488
or (800) 432-5566
for book order information

ABOUT THE ARTIST

Rod Cameron was born in 1948 in Chicago, Illinois, but has lived in Southern California most of his life. He studied painting with the "Dick and Jane" illustrator, Keith Ward, and at the Otis/Parsons School of Design in Los Angeles, California.

In 1985, Rod Cameron founded East/West Arts, Inc., a design and art studio in Ventura, California. His work has been shown on major network television and has received 17 awards for illustrative excellence.